Gracie with Flowers for You

GRACIE WITH FLOWERS FOR YOU

ISBN 0-85009-129-2 (Australia 1-86258-027-8)

Printed in Italy.
Worldwide co-edition organised and produced by Angus Hudson Ltd, London.

WORD PUBLISHING
Word (UK) Ltd
England

Word Books Australia, Sunday School Centre Wholesale South Africa, Alby Commercial Enterprises Pte Ltd Singapore, Concorde Distributors Ltd New Zealand, Cross (HK) Company Hong Kong, Eunsung Corp Korea, Praise Inc Philippines.

Gracie

BRINGS THIS BOUQUET OF GOD'S PROMISES TO BRIGHTEN YOUR DAY!

BE OF GOOD CHEER BECAUSE...

EPHESIANS 3:20

GOD IS ABLE TO DO
FAR MORE THAN WE
COULD EVEN ASK
OR THINK

DON'T LIMIT HIM!

PSALM 62:2

GOD IS YOUR ROCK,
YOU SHALL NOT
BE MOVED....

JUST STAND FIRM AND TRUST
HIM COMPLETELY

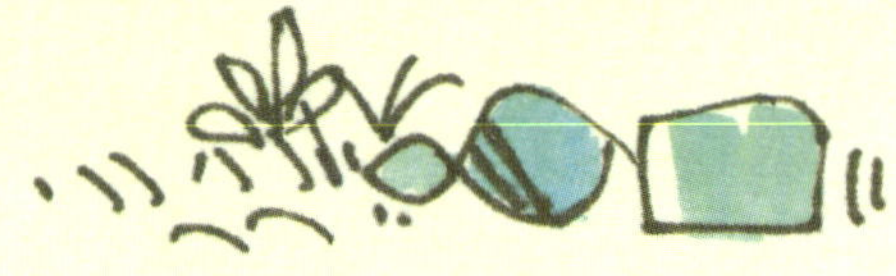

LUKE 12:6.7.

HE LOOKS AFTER THE SPARROWS ... AND YOU ARE FAR MORE VALUABLE

WITH TENDER CARE ...
HE WATCHES OVER YOU

PSALM 50:15

IF YOU CALL ON HIM
IN THE DAY OF TROUBLE
HE WILL
RESCUE YOU

HE WILL... HE SAID SO

ISAIAH 25:4

HE IS A REFUGE
IN A TIME OF
STORM

AND ... STORMS DO PASS
EVENTUALLY!

PSALM 147:3

HE HEALS THE BROKEN
IN HEART AND BINDS
UP THEIR WOUNDS

... EVER SO GENTLY

ISAIAH 58:11

THE LORD WILL GUIDE YOU
AND SATISFY YOUR
NEEDS ...
YOU WILL BE LIKE
A WELL WATERED
GARDEN

BLOOMING RIGHT WHERE
YOU'RE PLANTED

PSALM 37:7

YOU CAN REST
IN THE LORD
AND WAIT PATIENTLY
FOR HIM TO ACT.

KNOWING ... HE NEVER FAILS!

ROMANS 8:37

IN ALL THINGS WE
WIN VICTORIOUSLY
THROUGH HIM
THAT LOVES US.

NOT SOME THINGS ...
ALL THINGS!

WINNER

PSALM 13:5,6

YOU TRUST IN HIS
UNFAILING LOVE...
SING TO HIM
BECAUSE HE HAS
BEEN GOOD TO YOU

SING YOUR BLESSINGS

PHIL. 4:13

YOU CAN DO ALL
THINGS THROUGH HIM
BECAUSE HE
STRENGTHENS
YOU ___.

SO... GO FOR IT!

JOHN 14:18

HE WILL NEVER
LEAVE YOU
COMFORTLESS...
HE WILL COME
TO YOU

IN FACT... HE'S WITH YOU THIS MOMENT

BECAUSE HE LOVES YOU
AND HE WILL TAKE
GOOD CARE OF
YOU!